Beyond the Sky

Order by emailing fosterthomas094@gmail.com or call
225-425-2800

Dedication

To my (our) Lord and Savior Jesus Christ. He is faithful that promise. He is indeed the best person that has ever happen to mankind. We owe him all the praise, honour and glory.

To all of my children who are indeed a gift from God, I Love you very much Sheena, Terrell, Kimberly, Tia, and Caleb.

And of course my parents Thomas Foster III, Earlene Parker my wonderful and kind mother, my sisters Sonya Lamark and Lisa Foster and my brother Darryl Foster, my cousin Krystal Fleming, Laquan S. Whitfield, Aunt Jeannie "Betty" and Mary Foster, my loving and devoted wife

To my friends that are too many to mention, may God bless you all.

All of my nieces and nephews, Brandi, Tasha, Jeffery, Todd, Tonia, Kelsy, and Darryl Jr.

And of course the 5 amigos "The Hamilton Girls"

Table of Contents

Foreword

I want to take the time out to thank God for all his blessings he's done for me, my families life and continue to do. I'm not going to say I come from a poor family, but I didn't have much. We were raised to love each other and thank God for whatever and didn't complain about nothing. Coming up I was young when I had my first child. I left home at 17 years of age. It got really hard. I had too much pride to go back home to my mother's house. I lost two of my kids. One on April Fool's Day in 1999, and my daughter to domestic violence on November 26, 2017. She left behind 5 beautiful young girls ages ranging from 6-12 for me and my husband to raise. Sometimes we sit and try to figure out things that happen in our life, but I had to realize God don't make mistakes so I had to pray and let God do what he do. Everything seemed or looked bad for us. God meant it for good. A few years back I had a daughter diagnosed with Lou Gherig Disease ALS. The doctors said my child had six months to live. God have the last word on everything. She is walking and working today. The lord has blessed her with two beautiful kids. The doctor said 6 months but God said I have the last words. It has been 7 years. All the time God is good. I have seen God perform so many miracles in my life. All I can do is give him the praise. Don't get me wrong I'm far from perfect, but I do try to live and do the right things in life.

Always remember you have to pray, believe and have faith the size of a mustard seed. Ask and it shall be giveth. Knock and the door will be opened. Seek and you shall find. He heard my cry. Every day in my life the sun doesn't shine, the clouds get cloudier, and my heart gets a heavy burden, but I know who to call on. I look to the hill which cometh my health and strength which come from the lord.

James 1:22-But be ye doer of word, and not a hearers only deceiving your own self.

Mary Foster

Introduction

Life can be the most wonderful journey that one can embark upon . Because what I have discovered is it is not where we start but how we finish. This race is not given to the swift or strong but to those that endure to the end. When we run our race, patience is the key. I use to want everything "out of a microwave", quick, fast and in a hurry, but that's not how our heavenly Father work. Thank God for his patience and long suffering toward us.

You may be wondering why things sometimes happen the way they do and when they do, I can assure you he has a plan for your life (Jeremiah 29:11 KJV). The greatest thing that you can do is trust the Lord with everything that's in you. Why are you trying to figure it out? He has already worked it out. I wish I had known this in the beginning. I would have saved myself a lot of hurt and pain, but there is a process that we must all go through. Trust the plan of God for your life. He is there for you always, even when you can't sense his presence. He's right there watching how you will respond to what he allows in your life. That is the key to how you go in will determine how you come out. So lift up your head ole yea gates, and look toward the hill from which cometh your help, because all of our help comes from the lord. No matter what you're going through you can and you will make it in the name that is above every name the name of Jesus.

Chapter 1

The Beginning, Where it all started

Genesis 1

Reading the word of God in the beginning can be difficult. I remember as a child growing up that I knew that there was something different about me. I was what some people might call strange. Now there's a word that was not pleasant to hear, especially when you are a 12 year old boy who just wanted to be part of the gang. My friends and I loved to work on our bicycles and take long rides all the way across the other side of town. It was then that I knew that there was something different about me. I wanted to do more than ride my bicycle. I wanted to explore life. It was on journeys across town or around the world or just down the street to a neighbor's house is where we can begin our journey through life. In the beginning God created the heavens and earth "Genesis 1:2 KJV" the earth was without form and void and darkness was on the face of the deep, and the spirit of God was hovering over the face of the waters Vs 3. Then God said let there be light and there was light. "Genesis 1:1-3 KJV".

There I was feeling empty and void because I knew there was more to life, even at an early age. When we feel empty and void, there is room for God to come in and fill us with his presence. Life is more than having the material things that people crave today. There are a lot of rich people who have all the money in the world, and they are still not happy. Solomon said "whatever my eyes desired I did not keep from them. I did not withhold my heart from any pleasure. For my heart rejoiced in all my labor and this my reward from all my labor. Then I looked on all the works that my hands had done and on the labor in which I had toiled and indeed all was vanity and araspina for the wind. There was no profit under the sun". Ecclesiaste 1:10-11. The spirit of God was right in that we can obtain everything that our eyes could ever want, but at the end of the day we still feel empty. For what profit a man to gain the world and lose his soul? Or what will a man give in exchange for his soul? Matthew 16:26. Man has always sought after something. When we seek the kingdom of heaven and his righteousness, everything else will be addeth to him, and the Lord God formed man of the dust of the ground and breathed into his nostrils the breath of life, and man became a living being. Genesis 2:7. And in life there is a beginning and there is also an end. So we want to take you on a journey through life. If you ask most people today about their purpose or destiny in life, most of us don't have a clue.

To know God is to understand Him, and there is only one way to know the nature of God through his word. When we meet people there comes the point of getting to know that person. The reason most of us married the person we did is because we took the time to get to know them. We went on dates, we found out everything we could about them by communication. How can you know me if you don't communicate with me? You found out their favorite food, what movies they like, the color they like, kids etc.

The process can be lengthy. It can be life everlasting, but when you fall in love with a person, time is of the essence. There is no amount of time that we wouldn't be willing to devote to that person because a part of you longs to have a lasting relationship with them.

It can take and will take a great commitment to establish and maintain a great relationship. Once the relationship between two people is established, most would go to the end of the earth to take care and be with that person. No mountain could be high enough, no valley could be low enough for that person to conquest, "Therefore a man shall leave his father and mother and be joined to his wife and they shall become one flesh". Genesis 2:23 KJV

Once two people become one, they are inseparable. They become one with each other. They are indeed one, and there is nothing that will separate them. Then one day something very interesting happened in the Garden of Eden where God had formed man from the dust of the ground, later causing him to be put to sleep and brought forth woman from his ribs. Man was used to having a personal loving relationship with God. He was the greatest creature that He had made because he was made in his image and likeness. He loved us so much that he leaked apart of himself into man and we became a living soul. That's how much God loves us because we remind him of himself. That's why he gave us His only begotten son, that who so shall believe on Him shall have everlasting life. Jn 3:16.

"Now the serpent was more cunning than any beast of the field which the Lord God had made. And he said to the women," has God indeed said you shall not eat of every tree of the garden? And the woman said to the serpent, we may eat of the fruit of the trees of the garden, Genesis 3", but of the fruit of the tree which is in the midst of the garden. God has said, you shall not eat it, nor shall you touch it, lest you die, Vs 4. Then the serpent said to the woman, you will not surely die Vs 5 for God knows that in the day you eat of it your eyes will be opened and you will be like God, knowing good and evil. Vs 6 so when the woman saw that the tree was good for food, that it was pleasant to the eyes and a tree desirable to make one wise, she took of its fruit and ate. She also gave her husband with her and he ate. That moment was the beginning of the end for mankind. The loving relationship and fellowship that they once shared with God was over. They had become both physical and spiritually separated from God, all because they chose to disobey God. When we choose to disobey our heavenly father, there comes the void and emptiness in our heart.

The two greatest works that God has ever done was that of creation and that of redemption. There are no works greater than these. When that great act of what I call high treason was committed in the garden, when the fall of man and all of mankind had begun, it was then that the love of God was really put on display. It was at that moment that the heavenly council of God decided. He would offer up the only sacrifice that could redeem man back to God, the blood of Jesus. Yes, thank God for Jesus! Where would be like without him? The word of God says "when my father and my mother forsake me, then the Lord will take care of me." Psalms 27:10 KJV

Our heavenly father will always be there with us and for us, regardless of the lies that the enemy tells us. The same old lies that he spoke in the garden. As believers in the blood of Jesus,we have to reckon that that is just what he does. Tell the same old lies over and over again.

Jesus calls him at that moment the father of all lies, We cannot put any stock in what the devil does because he has transformed himself as an angel of light, but its not light that he wants to bring but rather deceit. He wants only to sever the relationship between us and God. That's his greatest desire, to put a wedge between man and God.

One may be asking why. I'll tell you it's because he's a hater. The only way that he thinks he can get to the Lord is by the people of God, because man is the most prized creation.

So, if he can put a wedge between God and man, he feel as though he can defeat. The great plan of God is to bring us together with him. The Bible says "for God did not send his son into the world to condemn the world, but that the world through him might be saved. "John 3:17 KJV"

Satan is the father of all lies, and he doesn't want you or I to know the truth about what the word of the Lord says as it regard our relationship with God. This is why we must study the word and know it for ourselves. His purpose is to deceive us just as he did in the Garden of Eden. "Genesis 3:1-7"

Chapter 2

"Where Art Thou "

Genesis 3:9

I remember a time in my life when things seemed as though they couldn't get any worse. I had gone through two divorces, my brother had passed, both sides of my grandparents had died, I lost my job, I had no where to stay, and to make matters worse satan was always whispering in my ear that I should give up and die because this God thing is not going to work for you. {Why do you keep trying to go on? You should just die and get it over with and make all things go away.} And if that wasn't enough, on November 12, 2012 my mother had a stroke. I was living in Colorado at the time the news came. One of my sisters called to tell me what happened. I almost dropped the phone. There I was feeling hopeless almost a thousand miles from my hometown of Baton Rouge, La. There was nothing else to do but pray. There are going to be times when the issues of life will hit us like a ton of bricks. It's in those moments and at that time that we have to put our faith and trust in God because there are things in our life that we have absolutely no control over. This was one of those times for me. "Proverbs 3:5" says trust in the Lord with all your heart and lean not on your understanding, in all your ways acknowledge him and he shall direct your paths. KJV

The scripture says to acknowledge Him. We should acknowledge Him in all affairs of our life no matter how small or how great. To include the Lord Jesus in all that we do will bring about a greater outcome because He knows what's best for us.

The holy spirit is so wise in all that he say and does. He is the perfect gentleman. He knows how to deal with each and everyone of us on an individual bases. We all have something different about us, it may be the color of our hair, the color of our skin or our religious belief, but how that God loves us all because the bible tells us that God is love, "for God so loved the world that he gave his only begotten son. That whoever believes in him should not perish but have everlasting life. "John 3:16 KJV"

It was this love that gave us a peace that passes all understanding. When we had gotten the news of my mother stroke, it was the love of Christ that kept her. It was the love of Christ that keeps you. It was that love that kept us and that led him to get together with the heavenly host where he would live a sinless life and go to the cross of calvary.

Thank God for the blood of Jesus Christ and him crucified, nothing but the blood of Jesus is what makes you and I whole today and the faith that's mixed with his word. One day there was a woman who had a issue of blood illness for twelve years. Now that's a long time to have a condition where she was alienated from everyone else, because she was declared unclean based on the belief of those around her. Oh how this poor lady must have felt.

No one to talk to, no one to pray with you, hug you or just hold your hand. But one day she heard that the one person who cares about us no matter what it is that we face was passing by. She said within herself, if I could but just touch the hem of his garment, I shall be made well. "Mark 5:28-34 KJV"

Sometimes our troubles and afflictions are not around us, but they are in us. You couldn't be able to say within it because the great hope of glory rest within each and everyone of us. Greater is he that is in us then he that is in the world. No matter how big the problem, God is greater. God is greater than any problem that has faced any man, woman, boy or girl on the earth.

Upon touching the garment she immediately felt the fountain of her blood dried up. Yes it dried up just like that, and she knew it because she immediately felt she was healed of her affliction. Vs 30 and Jesus immediately knowing in himself that power had gone out of him turned around in the crowd and said who touched my clothes? Now there were many people around him, and certainly a great number of people had touched him, but there was something different about this touch. It was a touch of hope and great faith. But more than that, it was a touch of life. She knew that if she didn't receive her healing by Jesus, she would be finished, and there would be no need for her to continue to live. She would have given up on life. And sometimes that's where most of us are in life, just like myself, losing all sense of hope, like we want to give up and throw in the towel. But praise God! He throws the towel right back, and says stay in the race because this race is not given to the swift or the strong but to the one that endures to the end. Thanks be unto God for keeping this lady in the race, for not giving up on her, but more important that she didn't give up. She kept fighting. She kept pressing forward pushing people out of the way. Stepping on anyone that would get in her way. Praise God this is the attitude that we must have, to never give up because it's never over until God say its over. And Jesus recognizing what had been done, looked around to see her who had done this thing. Vs 33. But the woman fearing and trembling knowing what had happened to her, came and fell down before him and told him the whole truth.

And he said to her, daughter your faith has made you well. Go in peace and be healed of your affliction. "Mark 25:34." Glory to God. One translation says that her faith has made thee whole.

In other words, not only did Jesus call her daughter which means that she want engravity in the family of God. Everyone else called her that woman because when you have an issue that's bigger than you, folks don't refer to you by your name. They just say you know that lady? You know that man that's been doing whatever or have whatever? And all of a sudden, you're labeled by your situation instead of who you really are. That's why I'm glad that God doesn't look at man the same way man does.

She was not only healed, but made whole. Not only was the fountain of her blood dried but (everything else that was wrong) Jesus made right. That's why it is important to wait on God's timing because he wants to do far more than we can ever see or even imagine. He wants to fix the whole picture. So no matter how bad it may seem on the outside, the son of man will always be shining on the inside. He is our bright and morning star, the offspring of David, the rose of Sharon, I could go on and on about who God is. Who is he to you? He should be everything all the time. Most times we call or pray to God when we need Him and then expect him to perform the miracle that we think that we need at that time. When it doesn't happen the way we think that it should or when it should, we get angry with God and draw back away to our own little world. "Psalms 34" declare "I will bless the lord at all times. His praise shall continually be in my mouth. I'm not just going to bless him when things are well, but at all times. Anybody can praise God when things are going well, but can you praise him when you have a condition like this woman or worse? I found out that's the best time to praise him. We praise him just because hallejuah. I don't need a reason. I praise and worship him just because he woke me up this morning, and I have the activity of my arms and legs. I can just clap my hands and stump my feet and sing not just a song but a new song, a song that even the angels can't. I am redeemed washed by the blood of the lamb.

He took my black sins, dipped them in his red blood, and I came out as white as snow. I used to wonder how can a brown cow eat green grass and produce white milk. Now I know, our God can do all things. He created the heavens and earth by speaking them into existence.

That's what we have to do to be able to speak the word of God over our situation.

Paul said "I think myself happy" Act 26:1," Life can be short, so don't waste anymore time holding your head down worrying about the things going on around you. God has everything under control. He knows what's going on far better than we do. Before I formed you I knew you in the womb. Before you were born I sanctified you. "Jeremiah 1:5." God has already walked our life out in the heavenly rim. This is just the manifested life here on earth. Enjoy life. Everyday that God gives us on earth is a day and time for us to fulfill our purpose.

Most people have asked the same question, because a lot of us have not discovered yet our real purpose in life. And your question may be what is my purpose, what is the plan of God for my life, what am I supposed to be doing.

Answer: That is a very valid question. A good one that needs to be answered, because we could wind up like the children of Israel who wonder in the wilderness for 40 years when the journey was only 11 days. Now where were they headed for 40 years, and what took them so long? There were several reasons for the long journey, but the main reason for their getting to their destination 4 decades later was because of their disobedience and their being rebellious to the voice of God. "Exodus 12".

Chapter 3

"The Plan of God"

When we choose not to hearken to the voice of god, then our journey too will become long and exhausting. But praise be unto God, even when we are at our worst, God is still at his best with us.

What is so amazing about the children of Israel. The God of Abraham, Issac and Jacob was there all the time. He never left them or forsake them because He is loving and compassionate.

The Lord has appeared to me saying yes, I have loved you with an everlasting love, therefore with loving kindness I have drawn you. "Jeremiah 31:3". Thank Jesus for drawing us back. What father or mother wouldn't love their child regardless of the mistakes that child has made? It doesn't matter about the decision they have made. They can always come back home to the parents. It's called unconditional love. Now grant it, it can be tough at times because we all want our children to do well and excel in life. What parent don't want that for their child?

When the prodigal son decided that he wanted his portion of goods right then and there, he had no idea what he was in for. Because he was anxious for it, it caused him more harm than good. And as a result, he not only lost his money, but nearly his inheritance. In other words, we can lose our place in the kingdom of God.

And he said to him, your brother has come and has received him safe and sound, your father has killed the fatted calf. "Luke 15:27 KJV". But he was angry and would not go in. Therefore his father came out and pleaded with him. Vs 29. So he answered and said to his father, Lo these many years I have been serving you, I never transgressed your commandment at anytime and ye you never gave me a young goat that I might make merry with my friends.

Vs 30-But soon as this son of yours come who has devoured your livelihood with harlots, you killed the fatted calf for him.

Vs 31-And he said to him, son you are always with me and all that I have is yours.

Vs 32-It was right that we should make merry and be glad for your brother was dead and is alive again, and was lost and is found. Praise God that's the love of the father. That not one should perish. God will go to great lengths to pull us up out of a situation, there is no amount of trouble in life that he will make uncomfortable for the love of another.

When we understand that our life is not our own, but Christ's, He will rearrange our life for the benefit of another. Just think, someone else's life was altered so that our life could be richly bless by the hands of someone else.

It's the power of love. Love is perhaps the most powerful tool that we have against the war of satan. That with faith in the cross of Jesus, when we began to love like Christ loves than we are able to withstand all that the enemy is trying to do.

Love unites not divides. Conquer love. Embrace not turn away love. Lift up not tear down. Love never fails. What a great world this would be if we were all able to experience the agape love of God. There would be no wars, famine, no hungry people, no homeless etc. The world would be a better place.

Back to what your purpose in life is. Many are still having a hard time trying to figure out what they are supposed to be doing, and a whole array of questions come along with that.

Most of us are deeply concerned with living meaning, purposeful lives. Unfortunately, our overarching purpose in life seems to have little to do with our circumstances. God's mission statement of sorts for our life doesn't include a graduate school title, well not directly.

It never starts with circumstances. It starts with his heart for all people.

So here it is. Drumroll please. When the holy spirit has come upon you, you will receive power, you shall be witnesses to me in Jerusalem and in Judea and Samaria, and to the end of the earth. "Acts 1:8 KJV"

When we commit our lives to jesus, we commit to an enduring, lifelong mission. We commit to a life of speaking, acting, thinking and relating out the transforming and joyful experience of being in a relationship with Christ. That's it. Wherever you are, whatever you think if it's the best fit or worst job ever, God wants to live out his mission.

The purpose for your life, the deepest place where you find meaning and satisfaction, transcends my role, job or circumstance you're facing. When jesus was here, he blew up everyone's paradigm on what it means to be purposeful and powerful.

He took the shadiest least likely characters, and made them powerful in his plan.

Yet we worry that what we are doing isn't meaningful enough, and we want God to change it like yesterday. It's easy for us to think that because we are children of God that all would be well. We think that we are suppose to get what we want. We already have developed a picture of what we want our lives to be like and believe that it's God's job to bring it to pass.

This is absolutely not the biblical picture of life with God, but a cheap version, a fake copy grown out of our self-centeredness. So here's a general idea of how this version usually develops.

1st-God saves me and offers me forgiveness and life. This must mean that he wants me to be happy and the way I plan it.

2nd-If hard times come this makes me question if God can be counted on.

3rd-If my picture of life is not coming true, it must mean that either God is punishing me or he is not who I thought he was.

4th-If tragedy happens, it must mean that God is either incapable or un-loving. Either he was not capable of stopping it which now means I have a crisis of faith, or he doesn't love me(or is punishing me or cursing me) which gives me an issue with my heart.

This version of Christianity is, first not Christianity at all. It is like comparing apples to oranges. There is simply no comparison.

19

How do we get out of impossible situations? When there is trouble on every hand, there is only one way out. You praise your way out.

(Beyond Circumstances)

Living with this make me happy. God is destructive to our joy and freedom in Christ. If we are constantly bound to the circumstances we believe we need in order to be joyful, we have become the lord of our own life. Believing our destiny is in our hands.
This creates a paralyzing insecurity that traps most of us in enslaving fear. No wonder we are so worried about wasting our lives. We are so busy trying to know God's plans that we are distracted from living them out.

God's ultimate mission statement for our lives doesn't mean he won't work to orchestrate relationships and circumstances (and yes even jobs that allow us to have meaningful experiences).

It's when we make those things the highest object of our devotion that we lose sight of what's really important. When we turn from our own ideas and commit our daily lives to his mission, we begin to walk more in step with him.

We then take the humble posture of believing that God has us where we are for a reason. Even as we take steps or work toward the next thing, we can keep our hearts present today.

We can ask God to let us be more concerned with his mission, and less concerned for ours. In doing so, we start to see the many ways God will be present, active, and engaged in our lives even if it's at the drive thru window.

The Lord will fulfill his purpose for me, your steadfast love o lord, endures forever. Do not forsake the work of your hands. Psalm 138:8. KJV

Chapter 4

The Mind Connection

Now that we have a better sense of what our purpose for God's life is (remember that our lives are his), we should take great pleasure in wanting for the Lord to fulfill his will in our lives. Life is not meant to be empty and void. There should be substance in our life.

I think that one of the keys to life is to fall in love with God. The word of God tells us to love the Lord with all of our heart. And to love him is to trust him. Trust in the lord with all your heart and lean not on your own understanding. In all your ways acknowledge him and he shall direct your paths. Proverbs 3:5-6

Women receive the last name of the man they dated after they get married. Once they are married she is entitled to everything that he has. It now belongs to her also because the two are now one. Well, can I tell you it is just like that with Christ.

We can't just date Him when we want to or want something from him. When we fall in love with Jesus and are married to him, when we are accepting Him as our Lord and Savior. That is, you confess with your mouth the Lord Jesus, and believe in your heart that God has raised him from the dead. You will be saved.

Vs 10-For with the heart one believes unto righteousness and with the mouth confession is made unto salvation. Roman 10:9-10 KJV

Praise God we then become married to God, and we are then given the power of attorney to use the name of Jesus. A name that is above all names, nor is there salvation in any other, for there is no other name under heaven given among men by which we must be saved. Act 4:12 KJV

The God Kind of Life

Let a man so consider us, as servants of Christ and stewards of the mysteries of God. I Cortinthians 4:1

What does it mean to live a life that's pleasing unto our heavenly father. Paul said in Vs 2 move over it is required in stewards that one be found faithful.

You see once one has been saved by the blood of Jesus (saved by faith), it is only the beginning. We have to be willing to be faithful to Christ. Like we indicated earlier, when a man and woman becomes one they are committed to each other. They are faithful to one another until death due them part.

And that's what God expects of us. He wants us to remain faithful to him regardless of what it looks like, regardless of what it sounds like. Loyalty to our heavenly Father is the most important part of our existence.

But without faith it is impossible to please him, Hebrew 11:6

Someone may be asking now, "what is faith"? That's another great question so I want to answer it from God's own words.

Now faith is the substance of things hoped for, the evidence of things not seen. Vs 2 "For by it the elders obtained a good testimony. Vs 3 "By faith we understand that the worlds were formed by the word of god so that the things which are seen were not made of things which are visible. "Hebrew 11:1-3".
Faith is our life line between heaven and earth. It is the one thing that God is moved by. A lot of people are under the notion that God is moved by the way we feel, what we think, how many tears we cry, etc. Although he is loving and concerned about how we feel, God is only obligated to his words.

If you want to get his attention, if you want the heavens to move on your behalf, began to speak the word of God.

The faith kind of life most often times we have the kind of faith that is put on display when we need something from God, but not for the advancement of the kingdom of God. It's the microwave type of faith, Lord I need you to move in this or that direction.

But what about when it pertains to the kingdom of God? Remember Joseph who had a dream one day, and his brother became jealous of him because of it. It was a dream from God, but his brothers were thinking the opposite.

"For behold we were binding sheaves in the field and lo, my shead arose, and also stood upright and behold your sheaves stood around about and obersance (bowed) to my shead". "Genesis 37:7 KJV". It was the will of God to relate this dream, which these brothers would remember and would see come to pass exactly as the dream proclaimed. He related this dream in the simplicity of his heart. And in doing, so he was also guided, unconsciously it may be but still really by an overruling providence who made use of this very telling of the dream as a step toward its fulfillment.

Vs 8-And his brethen said to him, shall you indeed reign over us? Or shall you indeed have dominion over us? They hated him yet the more for his dreams, and for his words. The answer to that question is yes indeed he would reign over them. Even while Joseph was in prison for the crime of rape, which surely never happened, he never lost his focus because through it all his faith in God remained intact. He was later made Prime Minister of all of Egypt, and his brother came and had to bow down to him just as God had given to him in his dream.

So no matter what it is that you are dreaming about doing, if it is God's will, it will come to pass. Don't ever let people dictate your destiny or your purpose in life. Throughout the whole story, God was at the helm of Joseph's life.

The Kingdom of God

We must display a faith that will propel us from the pits of slavery to the pinnacle of respect. Would you leave your front door open or your windows up in your home? No. Because if we did we would give the enemy every opportunity to come in and steal everything that we ever worked for.

It's the same way in the spirit realm. When we leave our spiritual gateway open to the enemy, he will come and rob us of the very thing that keeps us strong in Christ. The thief does not come except to steal, kill and to destroy. I have come that they may have life and that they may have it more abundantly. John 10:10 KJV

He want to steal the word of God from us because nothing else we have is of value to him. He can't drive, he can't cook and he certainly doesn't want to give God thanks. All he wants is your faith.

If we are to have victory in our lives, the one thing that we must do as believers more than anything else is to spend time with God. That's our life line. It's the only way to establish a relationship with him.

Stir up the hope that's in you. We can't get a drive through break through. God doesn't work like a microwave. He does things when it is time and not because we think it's time. He wants to give us a garment of praise for the heaviness. What an awesome God that is.

Bread just seems to taste better when it's fresh. Most of us want God to make the problems in our lives just disappear. But as a strong believer in the faith of christ, we endure like a good soldier. Paul had this same situation when he asked God to remove the thorns from his flesh, and lest I should be exalted above measure by the abundance of the revelations, a thorn in the flesh was given to me, a messenger of satan to baffled me, lest I be exalted above measure. Concerning this thing I pleaded with the lord three times that it might depart from me. And he said to me "my grace is sufficient for you, for my strength is made perfect in weakness".

Therefore most gladly I would rather boost in my infirmities, that the power of christ may rest upon me. 2 Corinthians 12:7-9 KJV

There you have it. The power of god is resting within us as we go through to get through.

Giant's do fall. The bigger they are the harder they fall. Giants show up to introduce you to yourself. If there would have never been a goliath, there would never had been a King David. " David put his hand in his bag and took out a stone and he slung it and struck the philistine in the forehead, so that the stone sank into his forehead and he fell on his face to the earth."

So David prevailed over the philistine with a sling and a stone and struck the philistine and killed him. But there was no sword in the hand of David. I Samuel 17:49-50 KJV

I would encourage you to read the whole chapter. It tells of how the hand of God plays an important role in the life of every believer. We have to trust God no matter what it looks like. No matter how great the giants are, they have to bow at the name that is above all names.

I've had many giants in my life. Just about everything that you can imagine, drugs, alcohol, bad marriages, in and out of relationships, the loss of one job after another, locked up, picked on, called every name that you can think of and the list goes on, but the one thing that I can say is that my relationship with God was still there.

Thank God for my family also. They have really been there for me through thick and thin. You know the ole saying, blood is thicker than water. Well my family has really been there with me through it all. When my brother Darryl passed 3 days before my wedding back in 1997, they encouraged me to go ahead with it. Then my grandparents on both sides passed and later on my father. We called him "Diamond" and he was just that a precious diamond, and now my mother "Earlene", she was the gem of the family, whom I miss dearly.

My two sisters Sonya and Lisa are the closet family that I have next to my heavenly Father. These ladies whom I love so dearly have always been there, even when the giants were there, they would stand with me until God defeated them.

Your family circle is the best circle to surround yourself with when trouble comes, and more than that, when it's not present. You want them to be present no matter what.

Someone maybe saying well my family doesn't care about me, or they don't love me because of what happened. There are many reasons why most families have been torn up, and the main one is that we allow Satan to come in and put a wedge right in the middle of us. That's what he wants to do divide and conquer.

But if we remember to always keep the man he was on the cross in the middle, which represented oneness. We can never be divided. A house that is divided against it. Self cannot stand.

So go and take your hammer as a tool against Satan and begin to rebuild everything that he has ever stole from you. Build your family back in Jesus name, and no weapon that is formed against you shall prosper. Isaiah

Take authority back over your marriage and your kids, your home and everything that God has given you.

When he has tried me, which implies the passage of time. There's no such thing as a quick way to refine gold. The process of refining, purifying and perfecting gold is a lengthy and painstaking process.

In the same way, God uses the painstaking process of our afflictions and suffering to refine and perfect his gold like qualities in us.

Job understood this, that his faith was being tested. (Job 23:1-10)

Faith must be tested. It's God's measuring tool to see where our faith really is. Great faith requires testing. Greater faith requires greater testing. When the test of severe trouble is applied and when man is thrown out of all conventional modes of thinking and speaking, the true character of the heart is revealed.

Jesus is our friend because a true friend will enter into the wilderness with you. A man who has friends must himself be friendly, but there is a friend who sticks closer than a brother. Proverbs 18:24

Beyond the Sky
(Final Destination)?

Chapter 5

Final Destination

It's amazing how when we look back on our lives we see how the development of things has change. I remember growing up from a little boy who at one time use to struggle just to tie his shoes to becoming an adult where I have to be able to maintain about all the responsibilities of life from bills to children to the careers and everything else that comes along with it.

We often look back and wonder where did all the time go. But what is more important than that, is how we spend our time that our heavenly Father has given us. We had just placed the headstone on my father's grave recently. Some of us are so consumed with the things of the world, we have forgotten all about our Father who is the giver of all things that pertains to life and godliness. What will people say about you in the end? What I have come to discover is that we will be remembered for two things in life, the problems we created and the one's that we solve.

God has a purpose for our lives, and I believe that is to do his will. Try and forget about what we want to do for a minute and focus on what he wants us to do. One of the reasons why I made so many mistakes is because I did what I thought to be right and not always living the way the word of what God says for us to. I Peter 5:6 KJV

Humble yourself therefore under the mighty hand of God, that he may exalt you in due time. In other words God's timing is the best timing. When we wait on him, we can rest assure that all things will work together for the good.

Our heavenly Father wants to exalt us- exalt means to raise something or someone to a higher place. The word of God says we exalt thee, O Lord. Psalms 30:1 When we raise him up, He raises us up. When we began to praise Him and thank Him for all that He has done. God begin to honor you in a way that will be hard for you and I to imagine, that's because He is awesome in who He is. He is the creator of heaven and earth. There is nothing too hard for him. In the beginning God created the heaven and the earth. And the earth was without form and void and darkness was upon the face of the deep. And the spirit of God moved upon the faces of the waters. And God said let there be light and there was light. Genesis 1:1

One word from God can change your direction. He spoke and everything came into existence. The one thing that I have discovered in life is that you may have a bad start, but you can have an awesome, victorious finish. Remember how Joseph had a dream, for behold we were binding sheaves in the field and lo my shead arose, and also stood upright and behold your sheaves stood around about, and made obeisance to my shead. And his brethen said to him, shalt thou indeed reign over us? Or shalt thou indeed have dominion over us? And they hated him yet the more for his dreams and his words. Genesis 37:7-8

His brethen take it very ill and more and more enraged against him. "Genesis 37:8" Shalt thou indeed reign over us? First see how they truly interpreted his dream that he should reign over them. Those become the exposiders of his dream who were enemies to the accomplishment of it, as in Gideon's story. (Judge 7:13-14) they perceived that he spoke of them. (Matthew 21:45)

The event exactly answered to this interpretation. (Genesis 42:6)

Second-How scornfully they resented it, shalt thou, who are but one reign over us who are many? Thou who are the youngest over us who are older? Note, the reign and dominion of jesus christ. Our Joseph, have been and are despised and striven against by a carnal and unbelieving world who cannot endure to think that this man should reign over the. The dominion also of upright in the morning of resurrection is thought of with the utmost dasdain.

Third-His father gives him a gentle rebuke for it, yet observe the saying (Genesis 37:10-11).

Probably he checked him for it, lessen the offense which his brethen would be apt to take at it, yet he took notice of it more than he seemed to do. He insinuated that it was but an idle dream because his mother was brought in who had been dead sometime since. Whereas the sun, moon and eleven stars, signify no more than the whole family that should have a dependence upon him and be glad to be beholden to him.

Note the faith of God's people in His promises is often sorely shaken by their faith.

But because we serve a God whose word is true, let the word of God penetrate your heart and begin to soak the deepest part of your spirit and take root in you so that it will begin to flow out of your belly.

Joseph let the word that God had spoken to him get in him and he responded to it. The word of God will never fail you. Begin to act on it. The faith that you have will produce the results that you want, and God has ordained.

Hold fast to the living savior the christ which has come and now is here no matter what you go through, no matter how many times you have been knocked down. If you can look up, then he will pick you. There's nothing that he can't handle. He is awesome, mighty, a strong towel. So let your journey be one of great hope. It may not have started wonderful like some, but it will end in victory when you reach beyond the sky.

Biography

Beyond the Sky is an introductory work by motivated speaker and Minister Thomas Foster IV also known to many as Main. He serves on the ministral staff of several churches where he attended. He was head coach of several little league BREC teams. He was born in Patterson, NJ with his family which later moved to Baton Rouge, LA where he spent most of his life with his two sisters and brother (deceased), father Thomas Foster III (deceased), and mother Earlene whom recently passed away.

Thomas Foster was a graduate of Delmont Elementary School and a graduate of Istrouma Senior High School, class of 81. He later attended Delta School of Business where he obtained a degree in Computer Programming. He later went on to complete and start his path that the Lord placed him on and graduated from the Bell Grove Seminary where he received his associated degree in Ministry.

He is the founder of Upon this Rock International Ministry. His prayer is that we should be all perfectly united in the faith of our Lord and Saviour Jesus Christ and that this work that God had given him through Beyond the Sky will help encourage you throughout your destiny and purpose that you have been assigned to and as always may the Lord continue to bless you always.

Thomas Foster IV

Prayer of Salvation

I hope that you have enjoyed reading some of what the Lord has placed in my heart. My hope is that if you don't know the Lord and are not Saved, here's the perfect opportunity to. This day can be the best day of the rest of your life.

According to Romans 10:9-13, That if thou shall confess with thy mouth, the Lord Jesus, and shall believe in thou heart that God hath raised him from the dead, thou shalt be Saved.

That is certainly good news. It's that simple, yet doesn't mean that all of your problems will go away, but it does mean that you have HIM there with you all the way.

If you prayed that scripture in your heart, congratulations! Welcome to the Kingdom of God.

Share the good news with me at fosterthomas094@gmail.com